AMERICAN BARD

AMERICAN BARD

WALT WHITMAN
THE ORIGINAL PREFACE TO LEAVES OF GRASS
ARRANGED IN VERSE, WITH WOODCUTS BY WILLIAM EVERSON
FOREWORD BY JAMES D. HART

THE VIKING PRESS | NEW YORK

Copyright © 1981 by William Everson
Foreword Copyright © 1982 by Viking Penguin Inc.

All rights reserved
This edition first published in 1982 by The Viking Press
625 Madison Avenue, New York, N.Y. 10022
Published simultaneously in Canada by
Penguin Books Canada Limited

A limited edition of this work was published originally by the Lime Kiln Press.

Library of Congress Cataloging in Publication Data
Whitman, Walt, 1819–1892.   American Bard.
    I. Everson, William, 1912–   II. Title.
    PS3201   1982   811′.3   81-68382
    ISBN 0-670-11706-4   AACR2

Printed in the United States of America
Book set in Monotype Goudy Newstyle

AMERICAN BARD
is dedicated to the memory of
Ralph Waldo Emerson
whose essay "The Poet" voiced
the unconscious aspiration
to which Whitman's ode
is the response.

*"I was simmering, simmering, simmering,
Emerson brought me to a boil."*

FOREWORD

Walt Whitman, the most comprehensive of American poets, introduced the first edition of *Leaves of Grass* with a lengthy prose text, ecstatic and transcendent, that announced a native view of poetry. The preface does not develop an argument, although it is full of striking phrases and moving images. Instead, it declares beliefs, themes, and attitudes that follow in the book's twelve untitled poems. More than half of these succeeding pages print the great fluid poem later known as "Song of Myself," whose long lines free of conventional metrical or stanzaic organization celebrate the unlimited potentialities of every person, conveying directly what the preface had only promised. Whitman presumably felt that the opening section of his volume of poetry was not a true preface for he never so titled it, and he dropped it from the second edition issued the next year. It did not appear again in the eight revisions of the ever-increased volume issued over the remainder of Whitman's life, although in time he salvaged some of the prose to be reworked into fragments of new poems added to the basic volume first printed in 1855.

Now, a century and a quarter later, William Everson, the poet from California who has long looked to Whitman as one of his masters, has revived this preface. Possessed of great passion and exaltation, Everson joined the Dominican Order as Brother Antoninus and then left it to express himself with intense appreciation of the human body and its powers. Though the course of Whitman's life was very different, similar drives animated him, and Everson is the kind of poet called for in the introduction to *Leaves of Grass*. At last, on the eve of his seventieth birthday, Everson has come into direct contact with Whitman, joining him to bring out the essential rhythms of his text.

The prefatory statement has seemed confusing because it lacks the progression of expository prose and it is inconsistent in tone: now oracular, now colloquial, and often composed of unpunctuated catalogs. The sentences, both run-on and abbreviated, are only loosely held together by dashes and three-period ellipsis marks.

But the prose comes alive when Whitman's rhapsodic tone and seminal statements are recast into poetic form. Everson has achieved this in a simple and direct way, for he only redivides lines and repunctuates Whitman's prose, altering neither words nor word order, to let its inherent poetry find full expression. Through this form of collaboration, Everson has made Whitman's preface more accessible, both emotionally and intellectually.

Everson has taken the original dozen tight pages of eight-point type set in rigid double columns and freed them typographically quite as much as he has opened them poetically. Of them he has made another long poem, as spacious as those that followed in Whitman's volume. Everson saw how to do this not only as poet but as printer, for he is a typographer of great accomplishment and distinction. Whitman, too, was both printer and poet (he set some of *Leaves of Grass* in type), but he was a mere journeyman whereas Everson is one of the few Americans of his time who has raised his craft to an art, as he works with type carefully composed by hand, solid ink long aged, dampened rag paper, and a nineteenth-century handpress. He knows how to achieve perfect harmony between text and typography, for his eye is as good as his ear.

Everson belongs to the great typographic tradition that has flourished during this century in the San Francisco Bay area. He is an inheritor of the bold style that the Grabhorn brothers and other Californians had used with their large typefaces marching across a folio page in masculine manner, accentuated by great initials in rich red or blue to contrast with the deep black of the basic lines. In his printing of *American Bard* Everson has used the same face and size—18-point Goudy Newstyle —that the Grabhorns selected in 1930 for their monumental presentation of *Leaves of Grass* in its final, fullest text. As Everson said, "It's the perfect type for . . . Whitman. When you lay ink on it with a roller, there's a certain surface tension that occurs between the texture of the ink and the face of the type." This tension remains imbedded in the paper. The striking Castellar initials used by Everson provide a strong counterpointed accent, as do the poet's woodcuts, one of a Whitmanesque bard whose full-bearded face symbolically encompasses a feminine profile.

The original edition of Everson's forceful printing of *American Bard* was on a rich handmade paper measuring a full foot by almost a foot and a half. This publication of the Lime Kiln Press, an adjunct of the University of California, Santa Cruz, had to be limited to but one hundred copies, for sale at a price appropriate to a work of art. The present trade edition, on a reduced but still generous scale, brings this poetic and printerly interpretation of a significant, neglected work of American literature within the reach of a large audience of serious readers.

—James D. Hart
Director of The Bancroft Library

AMERICAN BARD

AMERICA

Does not repel the past or what it has produced under its forms,
Or amid other politics or the ideas of castes or the old religions...

Accepts the lesson with calmness, is not so impatient as has been supposed
That the slough still sticks to opinions and manners and literature,
While the life which served its requirements
Has passed into the new life of the new forms...

Perceives that the corpse is slowly borne from the eating and sleeping rooms of the house,
Perceives that it waits a little while in the door, that it was fittest for its days,
That its action has descended to the stalwart and well-shaped heir who approaches,
And that he shall be fittest for his days...

THE AMERICANS, of all nations at any time upon the earth
Have probably the fullest poetical nature. The United States themselves
Are essentially the greatest poem. In the history of the earth hitherto
The largest and most stirring appear tame and orderly
To their ampler largeness and stir.

Here at last is something in the doings of man
That corresponds with the broadcast doings of the day and night.
Here is not merely a nation but a teeming nation of nations.
Here is action untied from strings necessarily blind to particulars and details,
Magnificently moving in vast masses.

Here is the hospitality which forever indicates heroes.
Here are the roughs and beards and space and ruggedness and nonchalance
    that the soul loves.
Here the performance disdaining the trivial—unapproached in the tremendous
Audacity of its crowds and groupings and the push
Of its perspective—spreads with crampless
And flowing breadth, and showers its prolific and splendid extravagance.

One sees it must indeed own the riches of the summer and winter,
And need never be bankrupt while corn grows from the ground,
Or the orchards drop apples, or the bays contain fish,
Or men beget children upon women.

9

OTHER STATES indicate themselves in their deputies,
But the genius of the United States is not best or most in its
executives or legislatures,
Nor in its ambassadors or authors or colleges or churches or parlors,
Nor even in its newspapers or inventors…but always most in the common people.

Their manners, speech, dress, friendships,
The freshness and candor of their physiognomy,
The picturesque looseness of their carriage,
Their deathless attachment to freedom,
Their aversion to anything indecorous or soft or mean,
The practical acknowledgement of the citizens of one state by the citizens
of all other states,
The fierceness of their roused resentment,
Their curiosity and welcome of novelty,
Their self-esteem and wonderful sympathy,
Their susceptibility to a slight,
The air they have of persons who never knew how it felt to stand
in the presence of superiors,
The fluency of their speech,
Their delight in music, the sure symptom of manly tenderness and native elegance of soul,
Their good temper and openhandedness,
The terrible significance of their elections,
The President's taking off his hat to them not they to him—
These too are unrhymed poetry.

It awaits the gigantic and generous treatment worthy of it.

THE LARGENESS of nature of the nation were monstrous
Without a corresponding largeness and generosity of the spirit of the citizen.
Not nature nor swarming states, nor streets and steamships,
Nor prosperous business, nor farms nor capital nor learning,
May suffice for the ideal of man—nor suffice the poet.
No reminiscences may suffice either.

A live nation can always cut a deep mark,

10

And can have the best authority the cheapest, namely from its own soul.
This is the sum of the profitable uses of individuals or states,
And of present action and grandeur, and of the subjects of poets.

As if it were necessary to trot back generation after generation to the eastern records!
As if the beauty and sacredness of the demonstrable must fall
    behind that of the mythical!
As if men do not make their mark out of any times!
As if the opening of the western continent by discovery,
And what has transpired since in North and South America,
Were less than the small theatre of the antique,
Or the aimless sleepwalking of the middle ages!

The pride of the United States leaves the wealth and finesse of the cities,
And all returns of commerce and agriculture,
And all the magnitude of geography or shows of exterior victory,
To enjoy the breed of fullsized men—
One fullsized man unconquerable and simple.

THE AMERICAN POETS are to enclose old and new,
    for America is the race of races.
    Of them a bard is to be commensurate with a people.
To him the other continents arrive as contributions.
He gives them reception for their sake and his own sake.
His spirit responds to his country's spirit.
He incarnates its geography and natural life and rivers and lakes.

Mississippi with annual freshets and changing chutes,
Missouri and Columbia and Ohio and Saint Lawrence with the falls, and beautiful
    masculine Hudson,
Do not embouchure where they spend themselves more than they
    embouchure into him.

The blue breadth over the inland sea of Virginia and Maryland,
And the sea off Massachusetts and Maine and over Manhattan bay, and over
    Champlain and Erie,

And over Ontario and Huron and Michigan and Superior,
And over the Texan and Mexican and Floridian and Cuban seas,
And over the seas off California and Oregon—
Is not tallied by the blue breadth of the waters below
More than the breadth of above and below is tallied by him.

When the long Atlantic coast stretches longer and the Pacific coast stretches longer
He easily stretches with them north or south.
He spans between them also from east to west and reflects what is between them.

On him rise solid growths that offset the growths of pine and cedar and hemlock,
And liveoak and locust and chestnut and cypress,
And hickory and limetree and cottonwood and tuliptree,
And cactus and wildvine and tamarind and persimmon,
And tangles as tangled as any canebrake or swamp,
And forests coated with transparent ice,
And icicles hanging from the boughs and crackling in the wind,
And sides and peaks of mountains,
And pasturage sweet and free as savannah or upland or prairie,
With flights and songs and screams that answer those of the wild-pigeon,
And highhold and orchard-oriole and coot and surf-duck,
And redshouldered-hawk and fish-hawk and white-ibis and indian-hen,
And cat-owl and water-pheasant and qua-bird and pied-sheldrake,
And blackbird and mockingbird and buzzard and condor,
And night-heron and eagle.

TO HIM the hereditary countenance descends, both mother's and father's.
To him enter the essences of the real things and past and present events,
Of the enormous diversity of temperature and agriculture and mines,
The tribes of red aborigines,
The weatherbeaten vessels entering new ports or making landings on rocky coasts,
The first settlements north or south, the rapid stature and muscle,
The haughty defiance of '76, and the war and peace and formation of the constitution,
The union always surrounded by blatherers and always calm and impregnable,
The perpetual coming of immigrants, the wharf-hemmed cities and superior marine,
The unsurveyed interior, the loghouses and clearings and wild animals
    and hunters and trappers,

The free commerce, the fisheries and whaling and gold digging,
The endless gestation of new states,
The convening of Congress every December,
The members duly coming up from all climates and the uttermost parts,
The noble character of the young mechanics and of all free American workmen
    and workwomen,
The general ardor and friendliness and enterprise,
The perfect equality of the female with the male,
The large amativeness, the fluid movement of the population,
The factories and mercantile life and labor-saving machinery,
The Yankee swap, the New York firemen and the target excursion,
The southern plantation life, the character of the northeast and of
    the northwest and southwest,
Slavery and the tremulous spreading of hands to protect it,
And the stern opposition to it which shall never cease till it ceases,
Or the speaking of tongues and the moving of lips cease.

For such the expression of the American poet is to be transcendent and new.
It is to be indirect and not direct or descriptive or epic.
Its quality goes through these to much more.

Let the age and wars of other nations be chanted,
And their eras and characters be illustrated, and that finish the verse.
Not so the great psalm of the republic.

Here the theme is creative and has vista.
Here comes one among the well-beloved stonecutters,
And plans with decision and science,
And sees the solid and beautiful forms of the future
Where there are now no solid forms.

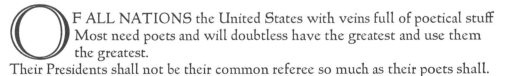

OF ALL NATIONS the United States with veins full of poetical stuff
    Most need poets and will doubtless have the greatest and use them
    the greatest.
Their Presidents shall not be their common referee so much as their poets shall.

Of all mankind the great poet is the equable man;

Not in him but off from him things are grotesque or eccentric or fail of their sanity.

Nothing out of its place is good and nothing in its place is bad.
He bestows on every object or quality its fit proportions, neither more nor less.
He is the arbiter of the diverse and he is the key,
He is the equalizer of his age and land.

He supplies what wants supplying and checks what wants checking.
If peace is the routine, out of him speaks the spirit of peace—
Large, rich, thrifty, building vast and populous cities,
Encouraging agriculture and the arts and commerce,
Lighting the study of man, the soul, immortality,
Federal, state or municipal government,
Marriage, health, free trade, intertravel by land and sea,
Nothing too close, nothing too far off—
The stars not too far off.

In war he is the most deadly force of the war:
Who recruits him recruits horse and foot.
He fetches parks of artillery the best that engineer ever knew.
If the time becomes slothful and heavy he knows how to arouse it.
He can make every word he speaks draw blood.

Whatever stagnates in the flat of custom or obedience or legislation,
He never stagnates: obedience does not master him, he masters it.
High up out of reach he stands turning a concentrated light, he turns the pivot
    with his finger.
He baffles the swiftest runners as he stands and easily overtakes and envelops them.
The time straying toward infidelity and confections and persiflage
He withholds by his steady faith, he spreads out his dishes.
He offers the sweet firm-fibered meat that grows men and women.
His brain is the ultimate brain.

He is no arguer, he is judgment.
He judges not as the judge judges, but as the sun falling around a helpless thing.
As he sees the farthest he has the most faith.
His thoughts are the hymns of the praise of things.
In the talk on the soul and eternity and God off of his equal plane he is silent.
He sees eternity less like a play with a prologue and denouement.
He sees eternity in men and women:

14

He does not see men and women as dreams or dots.

Faith is the antiseptic of the soul.
It pervades the common people and preserves them.
They never give up believing and expecting and trusting.
There is that indescribable freshness and unconsciousness about an illiterate person
That humbles and mocks the power of the noblest expressive genius.
The poet sees for a certainty how one not a great artist
May be just as sacred and perfect as the greatest artist.

The power to destroy or remold is freely used by him,
But never the power of attack: what is past is past.
If he does not expose superior models,
And prove himself by every step he takes,
He is not what is wanted.

The presence of the greatest poet conquers.
Not parleying or struggling or any prepared attempts.
Now he has passed that way, see after him!
There is not left any vestige of despair, or misanthropy or cunning or exclusiveness,
Or the ignominy of a nativity or color, or delusion of hell, or the necessity of hell.
And no man thenceforward shall be degraded for ignorance or weakness or sin.

THE GREATEST POET hardly knows pettiness or triviality.
If he breathes into any thing that was before thought small
It dilates with the grandeur and life of the universe.

He is a seer, he is individual, he is complete in himself.
The others are as good as he, only he sees it and they do not.
He is not one of the chorus.

He does not stop for any regulations, he is the president of regulation.
What the eyesight does to the rest he does to the rest.

Who knows the curious mystery of the eyesight?
The other senses corroborate themselves,

But this is removed from any proof but its own,
And foreruns the identities of the spiritual world.
A single glance of it mocks all the investigations of man,
And all the instruments and books of the earth, and all reasoning.

What is marvellous? what is unlikely? what is impossible or baseless or vague?
After you have once just opened the space of a peachpit,
And given audience to far and near and to the sunset,
And had all things enter with electric swiftness,
Softly and duly without confusion or jostling or jam.

THE LAND and sea, the animals, fishes and birds, the sky of heaven
and the orbs,
The forests, mountains and rivers, are not small themes.
But folks expect of the poet to indicate more than the beauty and dignity which
always attach to dumb real objects.
They expect him to indicate the path between reality and their souls.

Men and women perceive the beauty well enough, probably as well as he.
The passionate tenacity of hunters, woodmen, early risers,
Cultivators of gardens and orchards and fields,
The love of healthy women for the manly form,
Seafaring persons, drivers of horses, the passion for light and the open air,
All is an old varied sign of the unfailing perception of beauty,
And of a residence of the poetic in outdoor people.

They can never be assisted by poets to perceive: some may but they never can.
The poetic quality is not marshalled in rhyme or uniformity or abstract
addresses to things,
Nor in melancholy complaints or good precepts,
But is the life of these and much else and is in the soul.

The profit of rhyme is that it drops seeds of a sweeter and more luxuriant rhyme,
And of uniformity that it conveys itself into its own roots in the ground out of sight.
The rhyme and uniformity of perfect poems show the free growth of metrical laws,
And bud from them as unerringly and loosely as lilacs or roses on a bush,

And take shapes as compact as the shapes of chestnuts and oranges and melons
    and pears,
And shed the perfume impalpable to form.

The fluency and ornaments of the finest poems or music or orations or recitations
Are not independent but dependent:
All beauty comes from beautiful blood and a beautiful brain.

IF THE GREATNESSES are in conjunction in a man or woman it is enough,
The fact will prevail through the universe.
But the gaggery and gilt of a million years will not prevail.
Who troubles himself about his ornaments or fluency is lost.

This is what you shall do: Love the earth and sun and the animals.
Despise riches, give alms to every one that asks.
Stand up for the stupid and crazy, devote your income and labor to others.

Hate tyrants, argue not concerning God, have patience and indulgence toward
    the people.
Take off your hat to nothing known or unknown, or to any man or number of men.
Go freely with powerful uneducated persons, and with the young and with the
    mothers of families.
Read these leaves in the open air every season of every year of your life.

Re-examine all you have been told at school or church or in any book.
Dismiss whatever insults your own soul,
And your very flesh shall be a great poem and have the richest fluency,
Not only in its words but in the silent lines of its lips and face,
And between the lashes of your eyes, and in every motion and joint of your body.

The poet shall not spend his time in unneeded work.
He shall know that the ground is always ready ploughed and manured.
Others may not know it but he shall; he shall go directly to the creation.
His trust shall master the trust of everything he touches,
And shall master all attachment.

THE KNOWN universe has one complete lover and that is the greatest poet.
He consumes an eternal passion and is indifferent which chance happens,
And which possible contingency of fortune or misfortune,
And persuades daily and hourly his delicious pay.

What balks or breaks others is fuel for his burning progress to contact and amorous joy.
Other proportions of the reception of pleasure dwindle to nothing to his proportions.
All expected from heaven or from the highest he is rapport with,
In the sight of the daybreak, or a scene of the winter woods, or the presence
    of children playing,
Or with his arm round the neck of a man or woman.

His love above all love has leisure and expanse, he leaves room ahead of himself.
He is no irresolute or suspicious lover, he is sure, he scorns intervals.
His experience and the showers and thrills are not for nothing.
Nothing can jar him, suffering and darkness cannot, death and fear cannot.
To him complaint and jealousy and envy are corpses buried and rotten in the earth:
    he saw them buried.
The sea is not surer of the shore, or the shore of the sea,
Than he is of the fruition of his love, and of all perfection and beauty.

THE FRUITION of beauty is no chance of hit or miss.
It is inevitable as life; it is exact and plumb as gravitation.

From the eyesight proceeds another eyesight, and from the hearing proceeds
    another hearing,
And from the voice proceeds another voice eternally curious of the harmony
    of things with man.
To these respond perfections not only in the committees that were supposed to stand
    for the rest,
But in the rest themselves just the same.
These understand the law of perfection in masses and floods,
That its finish is to each for itself and onward from itself,
That it is profuse and impartial, that there is not a minute of the light or dark,
Nor an acre of the earth or sea without it—

18

Nor any direction of the sky nor any trade or employment nor any turn of events.
This is the reason that about the proper expression of beauty there is precision
    and balance.
One part does not need to be thrust above another.
The best singer is not the one who has the most lithe and powerful organ.
The pleasure of poems is not in them that take the handsomest measure
    and similes and sound.

WITHOUT EFFORT and without exposing in the least how it is done
    The greatest poet brings the spirit of any or all events,
    And passions and scenes and persons, some more and some less,
To bear on your individual character as you hear or read.
To do this well is to compete with the laws that pursue and follow time.
What is the purpose must surely be there, and the clue of it must be there,
And the faintest indication is the indication of the best,
And then becomes the clearest indication.

Past and present and future are not disjoined but joined.
The greatest poet forms the consistence of what is to be from what has been and is.
He drags the dead out of their coffins and stands them again on their feet.
He says to the past, Rise and walk before me that I may realize you.
He learns the lesson, he places himself where the future becomes present.

The greatest poet does not only dazzle his rays over character and scenes and passions,
He finally ascends and finishes all.
He exhibits the pinnacles that no man can tell what they are for, or what is beyond.
He glows a moment on the extremest verge.
He is most wonderful in his last half-hidden smile or frown.
By that flash of the moment of parting, the one that sees it
Shall be encouraged or terrified afterwards for many years.

The greatest poet does not moralize or make applications of morals: he knows the soul.
The soul has that measureless pride which consists in never acknowledging
    any lessons but its own.
But it has sympathy as measureless as its pride, and the one balances the other,
And neither can stretch too far while it stretches in company with the other.

19

The inmost secrets of art sleep with the twain.
The greatest poet has lain close betwixt both and they are vital in his style and thoughts.

THE ART OF ART, the glory of expression and the sunshine
of the light of letters
Is simplicity: nothing is better than simplicity.
Nothing can make up for excess or for the lack of definiteness.
To carry on the heave of impulse and pierce intellectual depths
and give all subjects their articulations
Are powers neither common nor very uncommon.
But to speak in literature with the perfect rectitude and insouciance
of the movements of animals,
And the unimpeachableness of the sentiment of trees in the woods
and grass by the roadside
Is the flawless triumph of art. If you have looked on him who has achieved it
You have looked on one of the masters of the artists of all nations and times.
You shall not contemplate the flight of the graygull over the bay,
Or the mettlesome action of the blood horse,
Or the tall leaning of sunflowers on their stalk,
Or the appearance of the sun journeying through heaven,
Or the appearance of the moon afterward,
With any more satisfaction than you shall contemplate him.

The greatest poet has less a marked style,
And is more the channel of thoughts and things without increase or diminution,
And is the free channel of himself.
He swears to his art, I will not be meddlesome,
I will not have in my writing any elegance or effect or originality
To hang in the way between me and the rest like curtains.
I will have nothing hang in the way, not the richest curtains.

What I tell I tell for precisely what it is.
Let who may exalt or startle or fascinate or soothe,
I will have purposes as health or heat or snow has, and be as regardless of observation.
What I experience or portray shall go from my composition without
a shred of my composition.
You shall stand by my side and look in the mirror with me.

20

THE OLD RED BLOOD and stainless gentility of great poets
Will be proved by their unconstraint. A heroic person walks at his ease
Through and out of that custom or precedent or authority that suits him not.
Of the traits of the brotherhood of writers, savants, musicians, inventors and artists,
Nothing is finer than silent defiance advancing from new free forms.
In the need of poems, philosophy, politics, mechanism, science, behavior,
The craft of art, an appropriate native grand opera, shipcraft, or any craft,
He is greatest forever and forever who contributes the greatest original practical example.
The cleanest expression is that which finds no sphere worthy of itself and makes one.

THE MESSAGES of great poets to each man and woman are:
Come to us on equal terms, only then can you understand us.
We are no better than you. What we enclose, you enclose.
What we enjoy, you may enjoy.

Did you suppose there could be only one Supreme?
We affirm there can be unnumbered Supremes,
And that one does not countervail another,
Any more than one eyesight countervails another,
And that men can be good or grand
Only of the consciousness of their supremacy within them.

What do you think is the grandeur of storms and dismemberments,
And the deadliest battles and wrecks,
And the wildest fury of the elements, and the power of the sea,
And the motion of nature, and of the throes of human desires,
And dignity and hate and love?

It is that something in the soul which says
Rage on, whirl on, I tread
Master here and everywhere,
Master of the spasms of the sky and of the shatter of the sea,
Master of nature and passion and death,
And of all terror and all pain.

21

THE AMERICAN BARDS shall be marked for generosity and affection,
And for encouraging competitors.
They shall be kosmos, without monopoly or secrecy,
Glad to pass any thing to any one, hungry for equals night and day.

They shall not be careful of riches and privilege; they shall be riches and privilege.
They shall perceive who the most affluent man is.
The most affluent man is he that confronts all the shows he sees
By equivalents out of the stronger wealth of himself.
The American bard shall delineate no class of persons,
Nor one or two out of the strata of interests,
Nor love most nor truth most, nor the soul most nor the body most.
And not be for the eastern states more than the western,
Or the northern states more than the southern.

EXACT SCIENCE and its practical movements
Are no checks on the greatest poet, but always his encouragement and support.
The outset and remembrance are there; there the arms that lifted him first
And brace him best; there he returns after all his goings and comings.

The sailor and traveler, the anatomist, chemist, astronomer, geologist,
Phrenologist, spiritualist, mathematician, historian and lexicographer are not poets.
But they are the lawgivers of poets, and their construction
Underlies the structure of every perfect poem.
No matter what rises or is uttered they sent the seed of the conception of it.
Of them and by them stand the visible proofs of souls.
Always of their fatherstuff must be begotten the sinewy races of bards.
If there shall be love and content between the father and the son,
And if the greatness of the son is the exuding of the greatness of the father,
There shall be love between the poet and the man of demonstrable science.
In the beauty of poems are the tuft and final applause of science.

GREAT IS THE FAITH of the flush of knowledge,
And of the investigation of the depths of qualities and things.
Cleaving and circling, here swells the soul of the poet,
Yet is president of itself always. The depths
Are fathomless and therefore calm. The innocence and nakedness
Are resumed, they are neither modest nor immodest.
The whole theory of the special and supernatural,
And all that was twined with it or educed out of it,
Departs as a dream. What has ever happened,
What happens and whatever may or shall happen,
The vital laws enclose all. They are sufficient
For any case and for all cases, none to be hurried or retarded.
Any miracle of affairs or persons inadmissible in the vast clear scheme,
Where every motion and every spear of grass, and the frames
And spirits of men and women and all that concerns them,
Are unspeakably perfect miracles, all referring to all,
And each distinct and in its place. It is also
Not consistent with the reality of the soul
To admit that there is anything in the known universe
More divine than men and women.

MEN AND WOMEN and the earth and all upon it are simply
to be taken as they are,
And the investigation of their past and present and future
Shall be unintermitted, and shall be done with perfect candor.
Upon this basis philosophy speculates, ever looking toward the poet,
Ever regarding the eternal tendencies of all toward happiness,
Never inconsistent with what is clear to the senses and to the soul;
For the eternal tendencies of all toward happiness
Make the only point of sane philosophy.

Whatever comprehends less than that,
Whatever is less than the laws of light and of astronomical motion,
Or less than the laws that follow the thief, the liar, the glutton and the drunkard,
Through this life and doubtless afterward,

Or less than vast stretches of time, or the slow formation of density,
Or the patient upheaving of strata, is of no account.

Whatever would put God in a poem or system of philosophy
As contending against some being or influence,
Is also of no account.

Sanity and ensemble characterise the great master.
Spoilt in one principle all is spoilt.
The great master has nothing to do with miracles.
He sees health for himself in being one of the mass.
He sees the hiatus in singular eminence.

To the perfect shape comes common ground.
To be under the general law is great for that is to correspond with it.
The master knows that he is unspeakably great, and that all are unspeakably great,
That nothing for instance is greater than to conceive children and bring them up well,
That to be is just as great as to perceive or tell.

IN THE MAKE of the great masters
The idea of political liberty is indispensable.
Liberty takes the adherence of heroes wherever men and women exist,
But never takes any adherence or welcome from the rest more than from poets.

They are the voice and exposition of liberty.
They out of ages are worthy the grand idea.
To them it is confided and they must sustain it.
Nothing has precedence of it and nothing can warp or degrade it.

The attitude of great poets is to cheer up slaves and horrify despots.
The turn of their necks, the sound of their feet, the motions of their wrists,
Are full of hazard to the one and hope to the other.
Come nigh them awhile and though they neither speak or advise
You shall learn the faithful American lesson.

LIBERTY is poorly served by men whose good intent is quelled
    From one failure or two failures or any number of failures,
    Or from the casual indifference or ingratitude of the people,
Or from the sharp show of the tushes of power,
Or from the bringing to bear soldiers and cannon or any penal statutes.

Liberty relies upon itself, invites no one, promises nothing,
Sits in calmness and light, is positive and composed, and knows no discouragement.
The battle rages with many a loud alarm and frequent advance and retreat.
The enemy triumphs, the prison, the handcuffs, the iron necklace and anklet,
The scaffold, garrote and leadballs do their work.
The cause is asleep, the strong throats are choked with their own blood,
The young men drop their eyelashes toward the ground when they pass each other.

And is liberty gone out of that place? No, never.
When liberty goes it is not the first to go nor the second or third to go.
It waits for all the rest to go: it is the last.

When the memories of the old martyrs are faded utterly away;
When the large names of patriots are laughed at in the public halls
    from the lips of the orators;
When the boys are no more christened after the same but after tyrants
    and traitors instead;
When the laws of the free are grudgingly permitted,
And the laws for informers and bloodmoney are sweet to the taste of the people;
When I and you walk abroad upon the earth,
Stung with compassion at the sight of numberless brothers answering our equal
    friendship and calling no man master,
And when we are elated with noble joy at the sight of slaves;
When the soul retires in the cool communion of the night and surveys its experience,
And has much ecstacy over the word and deed that put back a helpless innocent person
    into the gripe of the gripers or into any cruel inferiority;
When those in all parts of these states who could easier realize the true American
    character but do not yet;
When the swarms of cringers, suckers, doughfaces, lice of politics,
Planners of sly involutions for their own preferment to city offices,
Or state legislatures or the judiciary or congress or the presidency,
Obtain a response of love and natural deference from the people
    whether they get the offices or no;
When it is better to be a bound booby and rogue in office at a high salary
Than the poorest free mechanic or farmer with his hat unmoved from his head,

And firm eyes and a candid and generous heart;
And when servility by town or state or the federal government,
Or any oppression on a large scale or small scale,
Can be tried on without its own punishment following duly after,
In exact proportion against the smallest chance of escape—
Or rather when all life and all the souls of men and women are discharged
    from any part of the earth—
Then only shall the instinct of liberty be discharged from that part of the earth.

A S THE ATTRIBUTES of the poets of the kosmos
    Concentre in the real body and soul and in the pleasure of things
    They possess the superiority of genuineness over all fiction and romance.
As they emit themselves, facts are showered over with light,
The daylight is lit with more volatile light.
Also the deep between the setting and rising sun goes deeper many fold.

Each precise object or condition or combination or process exhibits a beauty:
The multiplication table its, old age its, the carpenter's trade its, the grand opera its.
The hugehulled cleanshaped New York clipper at sea under steam or full sail
    gleams with unmatched beauty,
The American circles and large harmonies of government gleam with theirs;
And the commonest definite intentions and actions with theirs.

The poets of the kosmos advance through all interpositions
And coverings and turmoils and stratagems, to first principles.
They are of use: they dissolve poverty from its need and riches from its conceit.
You large proprietor, they say, shall not realize or perceive more than anyone else.
The owner of the library is not he who holds a legal title to it
    having bought and paid for it;
Anyone and everyone is owner of the library who can read the same,
Through all the varieties of tongues and subjects and styles,
And in whom they enter with ease and take residence and force toward
    paternity and maternity,
And make supple and powerful and rich and large.

These American states, strong and healthy and accomplished,
Shall receive no pleasure from violations of natural models and must not permit them.
26

In paintings or mouldings or carvings in mineral or wood,
Or in the illustrations of books or newspapers, or in any comic or tragic prints,
Or in the patterns of woven stuffs, or anything to beautify rooms or furniture or costumes,
Or to put upon cornices or monuments, or on the prows or sterns of ships,
Or to put anywhere before the human eye indoors or out,
That which distorts honest shapes or which creates unearthly beings
    or places or contingencies,
Is a nuisance and revolt.

Of the human form especially it is so great it must never be made ridiculous.

Of ornaments to a work nothing outre can be allowed.
But those ornaments can be allowed that conform to the perfect facts of the open air,
And that flow out of the nature of the work and come irrepressibly from it,
And are necessary to the completion of the work.

Most works are most beautiful without ornament:
Exaggerations will be revenged in human physiology.
Clean and vigorous children are jetted and conceived
Only in those communities where the models of natural forms are public every day.
Great genius and the people of these states must never be demeaned to romances;
As soon as histories are properly told there is no more need of romances.

THE GREAT POETS are also to be known by the absence in them of tricks,
    And by the justification of perfect personal candor.
    Then folks echo a new cheap joy and a divine voice leaping from their brains:
How beautiful is candor! All faults may be forgiven of him who has perfect candor.

Henceforth let no man of us lie, for we have seen that openness wins the inner
    and outer world, and that there is no single exception,
And that never since our earth gathered itself in a mass
Have deceit or subterfuge or prevarication attracted its smallest particle,
    or the faintest tinge of a shade—
And that through the enveloping wealth and rank of a state or the whole republic of states
A sneak or sly person shall be discovered and despised;
And that the soul has never been once fooled and never can be fooled;

27

And thrift without the loving nod of the soul is only a foetid puff;
And there never grew up in any of the continents of the globe,
Nor upon any planet or satellite or star,
Nor upon the asteroids, nor in any part of ethereal space,
Nor in the midst of density, nor under the fluid wet of the sea,
Nor in that condition which precedes the birth of babes,
Nor at any time during the changes of life,
Nor in that condition that follows what we term death,
Nor in any stretch of abeyance or action afterward of vitality,
Nor in any process of formation or reformation anywhere,
A being whose instinct hated the truth.

EXTREME CAUTION or prudence, the soundest organic health,
Large hope and comparison and fondness for women and children,
Large alimentiveness and destructiveness and causality,
With a perfect sense of the oneness of nature
And the propriety of the same spirit applied to human affairs...
These are called up of the float of the brain of the world,
To be parts of the greatest poet from his birth out of his mother's womb,
And from her birth out of her mother's.

Caution seldom goes far enough.
It has been thought that the prudent citizen was the citizen who applied
    himself to solid gains,
And did well for himself and his family, and completed a lawful life
    without debt or crime.

The greatest poet sees and admits these economies as he sees the economies
    of food and sleep,
But has higher notions of prudence than to think he gives much
When he gives a few slight attentions at the latch of the gate.

The premises of the prudence of life are not the hospitality of it,
    or the ripeness and harvest of it.
Beyond the independence of a little sum laid aside for burial-money,
And of a few clapboards around and shingles overhead on a lot of American soil owned,
And the easy dollars that supply the year's plain clothing and meals,

28

The melancholy prudence of the abandonment of such a great being as a man is
To the toss and pallor of years of money-making, with all their scorching days
    and icy nights,
And all their stifling deceits and underhanded dodgings, or infinitesimals of parlors,
    or shameless stuffing while others starve,
And all the loss of the bloom and odor of the earth, and of the flowers and
    atmosphere, and of the sea,
And of the true taste of the women and men you pass, or have to do with in
    youth or middle age,
And the issuing sickness and desperate revolt at the close of a life without
    elevation or naivete,
And the ghastly chatter of a death without serenity or majesty,
Is the great fraud upon modern civilization and forethought,
Blotching the surface and system which civilization undeniably drafts,
And moistening with tears the immense features it spreads,
And spreads with such velocity before the reached kisses of the soul…

Still the right explanation remains to be made about prudence.
The prudence of the mere wealth and respectability of the most esteemed life
Appears too faint for the eye to observe at all, when little and large alike
Drop quietly aside at the thought of the prudence suitable for immortality.

What is wisdom that fills the thinness of a year, or seventy or eighty years,
To wisdom spaced out by ages and coming back at a certain time,
With strong reinforcements and rich presents, and the clear faces of wedding-guests
As far as you can look in every direction, running gaily toward you?

ONLY THE SOUL is of itself: all else has reference to what ensues.
    All that a person does or thinks is of consequence.
    Not a move can a man or woman make that affects him or her,
In a day or a month or any part of the direct lifetime or the hour of death,
But the same affects him or her onward afterward through the indirect lifetime.

The indirect is always as great and real as the direct.
The spirit receives from the body just as much as it gives to the body.
Not one name of word or deed; not of venereal sores or discolorations;
Not the privacy of the onanist; not of the putrid veins of gluttons or rum-drinkers;

29

Not peculation or cunning or betrayal or murder; no serpentine poison
    of those that seduce women;
Not the foolish yielding of women; not prostitution; not of any depravity of young men;
Not of the attainment of gain by discreditable means; not any nastiness of appetite;
Not any harshness of officers to men or judges to prisoners,
Or fathers to sons, or sons to fathers, or husbands to wives, or bosses to their boys;
Not of greedy looks or malignant wishes, nor any of the wiles practised by people
    upon themselves,
Ever is or ever can be stamped on the programme but it is duly realized and returned,
And that returned in further performances, and they returned again.

Nor can the push of charity or personal force ever be anything else than
    the profoundest reason,
Whether it brings arguments to hand or no.
No specification is necessary: to add or subtract or divide is in vain.

Little or big, learned or unlearned, white or black, legal or illegal, sick or well,
From the first inspiration down the windpipe to the last expiration out of it,
All that a male or female does that is vigorous and benevolent and clean
Is so much sure profit to him or her in the unshakable order of the universe,
And through the whole scope of it forever.

If the savage or felon is wise it is well.
If the greatest poet or savant is wise it is simply the same.
If the President or chief justice is wise it is the same.
If the young mechanic or farmer is wise it is no more or less.
If the prostitute is wise it is no more nor less.
The interest will come round, all will come round.

All the best actions of war and peace;
All help given to relatives and strangers and the poor and old and sorrowful,
And young children and widows and the sick, and to all shunned persons;
All furtherance of fugitives and of the escape of slaves;
All the self-denial that stood steady and aloof on wrecks and saw others take
    the seats of the boats;
All offering of substance or life for the good old cause, or for a friend's sake
    or opinion's sake;
All pains of enthusiasts scoffed at by their neighbors;
All the vast sweet love and precious suffering of mothers;
All honest men baffled in strifes recorded or unrecorded;

30

All the grandeur and good of the few ancient nations whose fragments
    of annals we inherit,
And all the good of the hundreds of far mightier and more ancient nations
Unknown to us by name or date or location;
All that was ever manfully begun, whether it succeeded or not;
All that has at any time been well suggested out of the divine heart of man,
Or by the divinity of his mouth, or by the shaping of his great hands;
And all that is well thought or done this day on any part of the surface of the globe,
Or on any of the wandering stars or fixed stars by those there as we are here,
Or that is henceforth to be well thought or done by you, whoever you are, or by anyone—
These singly and wholly inured at their time and inure now and will inure always
To the identities from which they sprung or shall spring.

Did you guess any of them lived only its moment?
The world does not so exist; no parts palpable or impalpable so exist.
No result exists now without being from its long antecedent result,
And that from its antecedent, and so backward,
Without the farthest mentionable spot
Coming a bit nearer the beginning than any other spot.

WHATEVER satisfies the soul is truth.
    The prudence of the greatest poet answers at last the craving
    and glut of the soul,
Is not contemptuous of less ways of prudence if they conform to its ways,
Puts off nothing, permits no let-up for its own case or any case,
Has no particular sabbath or judgment-day,
Divides not the living from the dead or the righteous from the unrighteous,
Is satisfied with the present, matches every thought or act by its correlative,
Knows no possible forgiveness or deputed atonement,
Knows that the young man who composedly periled his life and lost it
Has done exceeding well for himself, while the man who has not periled his life
And retains it to old age in riches and ease
Has perhaps achieved nothing for himself worth mentioning,
And that only that person has no great prudence to learn

31

Who has learnt to prefer real long-lived things,
And favors body and soul the same,
And perceives the indirect assuredly following the direct,
And what evil or good he does leaping onward and waiting to meet him again,
And who in his spirit, in any emergency whatever, neither hurries or avoids death.

THE DIRECT TRIAL of him who would be the greatest poet is today.
If he does not flood himself with the immediate age as with vast oceanic tides,
And if he does not attract his own land
Body and soul to himself, and hang on its neck with incomparable love,
And plunge his semitic muscle into its merits and demerits,
And if he be not himself the age transfigured, and if to him is not opened
The eternity which gives similitude to all periods and locations and processes,
And animate and inanimate forms, and which is the bond of time,
And rises up from its inconceivable vagueness and infiniteness
    in the swimming shape of today,
And is held by the ductile anchors of life, and makes the present spot
The passage from what was to what shall be,
And commits itself to the representation of this wave of an hour
And this one of the sixty beautiful children of the wave—
Let him merge in the general run and wait his development.

Still, the final test of poems or any character or work remains.
The prescient poet projects himself centuries ahead,
And judges performer or performance after the changes of time.
Does it live through them? Does it still hold on untired?
Will the same style and the direction of genius to similar points be satisfactory now?
Has no new discovery in science
Or arrival at superior planes of thought and judgment and behavior
Fixed him or his so that either can be looked down upon?
Have the marches of tens and hundreds and thousands of years
Made willing detours to the right hand and the left hand for his sake?
Is he beloved long and long after he is buried?
Does the young man think often of him? and the young woman think often of him?
And do the middle-aged and the old think of him?

A GREAT POEM is for ages and ages in common,
    And for all degrees and complexions and all departments and sects,
    And for a woman as much as a man and a man as much as a woman.
A great poem is no finish to a man or woman but rather a beginning.
Has any one fancied he could sit at last under some due authority
And rest satisfied with explanations, and realize, and be content and full?
To no such terminus does the greatest poet bring—
He brings neither cessation or sheltered fatness and ease.
The touch of him tells in action. Whom he takes
He takes with firm sure grasp into live regions previously unattained—
    thenceforward is no rest—
They see the space and ineffable sheen that turn the old spots and lights
    into dead vacuums.
The companion of him beholds the birth and progress of stars
    and learns one of the meanings.
Now there shall be a man cohered out of tumult and chaos.
The elder encourages the younger and shows him how.
They two shall launch off fearlessly together till the new world fits an orbit for itself,
And looks unabashed on the lesser orbits of the stars,
And sweeps through the ceaseless rings, and shall never be quiet again.

THERE WILL SOON be no more priests: their work is done.
    They may wait awhile, perhaps a generation or two, dropping off by degrees.
    A superior breed shall take their place;
The gangs of kosmos and prophets en masse shall take their place.
A new order shall arise and they shall be the priests of man,
And every man shall be his own priest.
The churches built under their umbrage shall be the churches of men and women.
Through the divinity of themselves shall the kosmos, and the new breed of poets,
Be interpreters of men and women, and of all events and things.
They shall find their inspiration in real objects today, symptoms of the past and future.
They shall not deign to defend immortality or God, or the perfection of things,
Or liberty or the exquisite beauty and reality of the soul.
They shall arise in America, and be responded to from the remainder of the earth.

THE ENGLISH LANGUAGE befriends the grand American expression.
It is brawny enough and limber and full enough.
On the tough stock of a race who through all change of circumstances
Was never without the idea of political liberty, which is the animus of all liberty,
It has attracted the terms of daintier and gayer and subtler and more elegant tongues.
It is the powerful language of resistance; it is the dialect of common sense.
It is the speech of the proud and melancholy races and of all who aspire.
It is the chosen tongue to express growth, faith, self-esteem,
Freedom, justice, equality, friendliness, amplitude, prudence, decision and courage.
It is the medium that shall well nigh express the inexpressible.

NO GREAT LITERATURE, nor any like style of behavior or oratory
Or social intercourse or household arrangements or public institutions,
Or the treatment by bosses of employed people,
Nor executive detail or detail of the army or navy,
Nor spirit of legislation or courts or police or tuition,
Or architecture or songs or amusements or the costumes of young men,
Can long elude the jealous and passionate instinct of American standards.

Whether or no the sign appears from the mouths of the people,
It throbs a live interrogation in every freeman's and freewoman's heart,
After that which passes by or this built to remain.
Is it uniform with my country? Are its disposals without ignominious distinctions?
Is it for the evergrowing communes of brothers and lovers,
Large, well-united, proud beyond the old models, generous beyond all models?
Is it something grown fresh out of the fields or drawn from the sea
    for use to me today here?

I know that what answers for me, an American,
Must answer for any individual or nation that serves for a part of my materials.
Does this answer? Or is it without reference to universal needs?
Or sprung of the needs of the less developed society of special ranks?
Or old needs of pleasure overlaid by modern science and forms?
Does this acknowledge liberty with audible and absolute acknowledgement,
And set slavery at nought for life and death?

Will it help breed one good-shaped and well-hung man,
And a woman to be his perfect and independent mate?
Does it improve manners? Is it for the nursing of the young of the republic?
Does it solve readily with the sweet milk of the nipples of the breasts
    of the mother of many children?
Has it too the old ever-fresh forbearance and impartiality?
Does it look with the same love on the last born,
And on those hardening toward stature, and on the errant, and on those
Who disdain all strength of assault outside of their own?

THE POEMS DISTILLED from other poems will probably pass away.
The coward will surely pass away.
The expectation of the vital and great
Can only be satisfied by the demeanor of the vital and great.

The swarms of the polished deprecating and reflectors and the polite
    float off and leave no remembrance.
America prepares with composure and goodwill for the visitors that have sent word.
It is not intellect that is to be their warrant and welcome.
The talented, the artist, the ingenious, the editor, the statesman, the erudite—
They are not unappreciated; they fall in their place and do their work.

The soul of the nation also does its work.
No disguise can pass on it, no disguise can conceal from it.
It rejects none, it permits all.
Only toward as good as itself and toward the like of itself will it advance halfway.
An individual is as superb as a nation when he has the qualities which make a superb nation.
The soul of the largest and wealthiest and proudest nation may well go halfway
    to meet that of its poets.
The signs are effectual. There is no fear of mistake. If the one is true the other is true.
The proof of a poet is that his country absorbs him as affectionately as he has absorbed it.

35

NOTE

This work stands witness to the printer's conviction that Whitman's Preface to the first edition of "Leaves of Grass" is essentially a poem. Written in the creative exaltation following the breakthrough emergence of his seminal masterpiece, it partakes of the same vital energy. Its intrinsically poetic substance may be surmised from the fact that an estimated forty-three percent of the text, whole paragraphs as well as individual lines, found its way into subsequent poems. Principal among these is "By Blue Ontario's Shore," which has been called the "poetical equivalent of the 1855 Preface." But that work is a patent amalgam which in no way realizes the unity and cumulative force of the original.

Why Whitman never realized this remains unexplained, but since he dismissed the piece as of little worth (a judgment in which posterity has not concurred) it is assumed he was embarrassed by its obvious derivation from Emerson's famous essay "The Poet." But he need not have been troubled by its source, for such is its vision that it soars into another dimension. Long celebrated among Whitman's prose pieces for its vigor, it resists assimilation into that genre. Arranged as prose, its inversions clog, its rhythms fight themselves. Arranged as verse, they soar, proclaiming the presence of an unacknowledged masterpiece of American poetry.

The text is that of the original edition, with spelling modernized and punctuation adapted, but the order of Whitman's words is left unchanged. May the reader experience the excitement and quickening involvement the printer felt in first liberating its lines.

W.E.

WILLIAM EVERSON was born in 1912 in Sacramento, California, and grew up in Selma in the San Joaquin Valley, where his father was a printer and musician. He briefly attended Fresno State College, dropping out to go back to the land and pursue a vocation as a poet. He served as a conscientious objector in World War II and at war's end gravitated to the Bay Area to join the nucleus of the San Francisco Renaissance, a catalyst for the Beat Generation. In 1949 he converted to Catholicism, and in 1951 he entered the Dominican Order and took the name Brother Antoninus. In 1969, after eighteen years as a lay brother, he left the Dominicans to marry. Everson has published over forty books of poetry and scholarship and is a hand-press printer of distinction. His honors include a Guggenheim Fellowship in 1949, a Pulitzer Prize nomination in 1959, the silver Medal of the Commonwealth Club in 1967, and the Shelley Memorial Award in 1978. He currently lives with his wife and son in the mountains near the University of California, Santa Cruz, where he has been poet in residence since 1971.

JAMES D. HART is a professor at the University of California, Berkeley, where he teaches courses on American literature. He is also director of The Bancroft Library, the campus's collection of rare books and Western Americana. He has published several books, including *A Companion to California, The Oxford Companion to American Literature,* and *The Popular Book: A History of America's Literary Taste.*